—— THE ——
DECISION

PAUL R. WIESENFELD

Leavitt Peak Press

ISBN: 978-1-964462-55-4 (sc)
ISBN: 978-1-964462-56-1 (e)

Rev. date: 07/15/2024

THE DECISION

This is the story of Alan Gompers having to make a life altering "decision". A decision of such magnitude that it is now simply known as *"the decision"*.

On a startlingly clear spring day in 1981, Alan drove his brand, new Cadillac Eldorado onto his estate believing he was home safe. Sure, he had a rough day but it was also exciting, challenging and just dangerous enough to give him the constant thrill he needed. I got this figured out, he thought. No one knows where I go, what I do or how I do it.

Just as he stopped the car and opened the door to get out, he heard the screeching tires, sirens and then, a police officer screaming "put your hands on your head, get on the ground" and then the words he feared the most, "you're under arrest". Suddenly he felt a gun jammed against his head. Only this time, it was not a police officer but a very large and angry detective who started speaking to him in a sneering vulgar manner. "We got you sucker; you're going away for the rest of your sorry life. Don't move or I'll splatter your brains all over this car".

The warm spring day turned into a dark cold winter night. The outside temperature of 68 degrees seemed to drop to ice cold, his whole body shivered. Fear, an otherwise unknown companion, suddenly engulfed every fiber in his being. This new companion spoke to him in a calm, clear yet unequivocal voice" I will be with you Alan, all the time now, wherever you go, no matter what you do or who you're with".

Alan knew one day this could happen but the drugs he took, then sold, spoke to him, saying, "don't worry you won't get caught, you're too good, you're too smart, you're safe, just keep using and everything will be all right".

In a crisis like this, time slows perceptively. However, he realized his worst nightmare was coming true and time began to speed up so much he could hardly breathe, think, or see clearly. All he knew was that some very strong detective was commanding him now to put his hands behind his back and to put his face on the hood of the car. The demanding tone of this detective, as well as the gun placed to Alan's head so immobilized him, he simply obeyed.

As the handcuffs were clasped on his wrists, a strong hand pushed his face to the hood of the car. Alan heard the detective say "don't move, just listen to me". Alan tried to calm himself but the effort was useless. The detective, believing he had accomplished his goal, turned Alan around so they were face to face. He looked at Alan as if he were a piece of trash ready to be discarded and said, "we got you shit bag". After moving closer to Alan said, "you're nothing but a fucking drug dealer, you're going to jail for the rest of your life", yeah, the rest of your life".

They looked at each other, eye to eye, then the detective released his grip from Alan's throat collar and smiled as if all this was over and said disingenuously "do you understand what I just said?" Then the detective paused, looked Alan in the eye (harder than before), and suddenly screamed at him, with his face just 6 inches from Alan saying, "do you"?

Alan was so startled by the sound of the detective's voice, he tried to recoil in horror but as his back was against the hood of the car, no movement was possible. His mind suddenly broke free from the fog of fear and a clarity of awareness descended upon him the likes of which he had never known. His heart, all the while beating like a drum, slowed to a gentle tapping. His thoughts, which were once racing, had now slowed to a gradual murmur. Yes, he said to himself, I understand, I know exactly what is happening to me.

Alan did not respond verbally to the detective's entreaties, he merely obeyed. Alan knew something worse was coming because the detective gave it away by smiling and releasing his grip. Alan, he said, "your life is over. You have no hope of winning, no chance to escape. You're mine. The future for you is jail where they will make you "a bitch" so get used to nothing but pain and suffering".

The detective thought he knew what the impact would be to Alan as he had done this several times before and gotten the results he wanted. He paused for effect, looked at Alan and said (this time in a calm measured voice) "do you want this? is this what you want"? without saying a word, with the steadiness of his eyes only, Alan communicated with the detective, implying "go ahead, tell me, I'm ready".

The detective moved in closer and whispered in his ear so the other police officers could not hear "if you give me the name and address of your supplier, we can make a deal. If you will accept it, you can go home now, you will be free, no jail". What to do? Alan was given a choice-- one he never thought he would have to make and now he had to decide. The detective wanted him to decide right now.

Alan wanted to say just what the detective wanted to hear. He wanted to end this traumatic situation as quickly as he could. Yet something somewhere deep inside him said wait a minute hold on, be silent there may be another path to follow. The very thought of going to prison for the rest of his life was a torment he thought he could not bear but at the same time, he also knew what might happen to him if he gave up the name of his supplier.

He imagined his wife coming over and saying. Alan, I love you. I need you to give the detective what he wants. This would be too easy he thought but yes, he so much wanted to take her advice. Troubled, he thought of Wisey--his good friend, and wanted to ask him but he was not offered a phone call or even the advice of a lawyer.

As these conflicting thoughts were waging war in his head, there was a slight movement of the detective's body and he said "oh I should tell you, dirt bag, you have the right to remain silent, you also have the right to a lawyer and if you cannot afford one, some public defender will help you out". At that very instant, Alan had the answer he needed. I'll ask for a lawyer and remain silent. This will give me time to think. He knew he did not have a lot of time but at least he was given some time and he needed all the time he could get.

HISTORY AND BACKGROUND

To appreciate the how, and the why which led Alan to make the decision he made, we first have to look at who he was growing up. He grew up in Parkchester, "Da Bronx" in the 40's and 50's. It was a middle class, white, Italian, Jewish and Irish neighborhood. His parents were, as were every parent in Parkchester, struggling to make it economically. Parkchester was a huge complex of apartment houses, parks and playgrounds built by Metropolitan Life Insurance Company.

Alan's performance in just about everything he did was barely average. He was somewhat popular, but otherwise, average in sports, friends and school. The only talent he showed that separated him from everyone else, was in music. In this category, he was so good, he was accepted at the High School of Music and Art, in Manhattan.

In the early 50's, doo wop music became the rage and as it turned out, Alan could sing, and sing he did. He even formed a group of "doo wop" singers who sang in the moonlight, on street corners and in High School halls. The "Moderniers" was the name of his group. They had only one, semi-hit. Agents in those days knew how to take advantage of talented minors for their profit. And because of that exploitation, the Modernairs made little to no money while the manager and producer got it all.

TRAIN RIDE

The first real glimpse we get of who and what Alan was, occurred during the train ride he, Wisey and Billy took in the summer of '54. The three teenagers rode the subway from Parkchester, "Da Bronx" to lower Manhattan, where they had summer jobs at the New York State Insurance Fund.

Just sitting on a train for an hour until it stopped in lower Manhattan was boring and uneventful. The ride had no excitement, no drama and no surprises for the young teenage boys. Alan, all of 16 at the most, looked for something to do or he thought he would die of boredom. And find it, he did.

In those days, the rear door of the train closed with a rubber stopper at the end. Alan, seeing this and realizing its elasticity, tried to put his hand out of the door through the rubber stopper. He was successful. No one had ever thought to do this, but Alan saw his chance to create some mayhem and told Wisey and Billy of his idea for a prank.

As the train pulled away from the stop, people were standing on the platform reading newspapers. Alan stood by the rear door and stuck his hand out through the rubber stopper and pulled a newspaper "out from" someone's hand while they were reading it holding it upright. The train pulled away with their newspaper flapping out from the rear car door. The look of astonishment and bewilderment on the face of the person who just had his newspaper snatched, sent gales of laughter to Alan, Wisey and Billy. What could the person do? Suddenly, they had no newspaper and no way to chase after the train as it pulled away.

THE FIGHT

As summer ended and school started for the 3 teenagers, each went to a different High School. Wisey went to James Monroe, Billy went to, The Bronx High School of Science, and Alan to the High School of Music and Art. All 3 teens were different, yet the same in a great many respects- Billy was the smart one, Wisey the athlete, and Alan the musician.

One day in early September an Irish kid in Wisey's English class for no discernable reason started a fight with him. Most likely because he was Jewish. Wisey was not a tough kid or one who looked for trouble. The Irish kid however lost the fight but got his older brother to come to avenge his travail. The older brother who was in a gang and was bigger, and stronger than Wisey, and when he saw Wisey, he realized an opportunity for his gang "The Archer Street Thugs" to challenge a bunch of Jewish kids to a fight, which he knew his gang would win.

Wisey had no gang, was not interested in fighting but was shamed by the challenge and knew he had to go or else be labeled a coward. He asked his friends to come and defend him but one by one, they offered the lamest of excuses, e.g., "I can't go with you", "I have to watch TV", "my mother said I can't get my new shirt dirty" and the most popular, I have to study for a test".

At the appointed time and place, Wisey showed up only to find just one person there to help   defend him and that person was Alan. The two of them stood shoulder to shoulder as the dreaded Archer Street Thugs came forward., It seemed to Alan and Wisey there were at least 10,000 of them. However, since it was only Wisey and Alan, the fight was so unfair, so unsupportable, the Archer Street Thugs did not know what to do. They could not just go home and be shamed by two little Jewish kids. They had to do something, but what?

When the biggest of the older brothers stepped forward and challenged Wisey to a fight, Alan reacted and punched the guy in the nose starting a free for all with10,000 Irish kids jumping on the two of them. Luckily the Parkchester police, the Good Humor ice cream man and a street cleaner came and broke up the mele. Alan and Wisey ran home to Wisey's apartment where his mother comforted them with praise and condolences.

News of Alan's bravery in this mele spread like a wildfire among the Parkchester residents. He became the talk of Parkchester in general and the teens' parents. Everyone knew only Alan had the courage to come help Wisey. Only Alan stood by Wisey's side. Alan demonstrated a fearlessness, a bravery, and courage no one else had. Alan stood out among all of Wisey's friends. He was a hero of epic proportions in the eyes of all teenagers and parents in Parkchester.

Why did Alan show up while none of Wisey's other friends would come? Why did Alan stand with him and defend him when no one else would? What made Alan come and face the Archer Street

Thugs having no regard for his own personal safety? Something deep and profound within him was expressing itself and no one, let alone Alan, knew what it was. The answer to these questions portends the dramatic making by Alan of *"the decision"*.

FIFTEEN YEARS LATER ALAN AND A NEW FRIEND ENTER THE STOCK MARKET

The preceding 15 years were quiet, if not dull, for Alan. He did not find himself or a direction that would give him the excitement for which he clamored. He graduated from Hunter College (barely) and then taught physical education on a High School level, worked at the Catskill mountains in the summer and seemed destined for a normal, safe, easy life until his new friend Howie, got him interested in the stock market.

Howie was the moving force here but Alan carried his share of the load. They were not gifted analysts of market trends rather they were great at "selling". And selling stocks was just what they did. Eventually, they were so good they became partners in a small over-the-counter stock company. It was here that Howie figured out how to make a lot of money quickly, and wrongfully.

Together they made a fortune by cheating and scamming clients, friends and family alike. Money rolled in the likes of which he only dreamed of. But while Alan was getting very comfortable financially, and seemingly having it all, he was losing his boundaries, his self-respect, and his friends. He could not trust anyone any more as everyone only wanted his money not his friendship. He only had one friend—Wisey—who while distant, was in awe of his success but feared for Alan's prospects.

Making so much money with so little effort gave Alan ostensibly what he thought he wanted however, it also brought home more trouble than he could ever have imagined. He was losing his bearings all the while gaining material things. He had new and better cars, a new and better home. His marriage and kids were secondary but they did provide some comfort. Nothing it seemed, stemmed his slide downwards to emotional insecurity. The path to financial success seemed open and far too easy but with it came something new and incredibly powerful "fear".

The more money Alan made the worse his life became. Sure, he had cars, took lavish vacations bought whatever clothes he wanted; but he had no center, no sure and safe path to follow. It seemed to him that he had to keep doing what he was doing even though he knew it was wrong.

Howie taught him how to steal, cheat and use others for financial gain. Alan wanted his friendship, and he wanted the money but not at the cost of losing everything else he held dear. It seemed to him it was too late to change and he was right. It was too late he just didn't know it for sure. Yet, something deep down inside him said they could not keep getting away with what they were doing; and sure enough one day the Attorney General of NY came knocking at their door. The knock was a hard one but just and fair.

PLEADING GUILTY

This criminal matter, the first for Alan, was traumatic to be sure, but he and Howie were of the belief they were invincible. The fear that should have guided him and controlled his senses was lacking. He was sure they would beat the rap. Unfortunately, as it turned out they did beat the rap as they only got probation, a fine and 10 hours of ethics training. They did not learn the needed lesson.

Alan knew, deep down inside that something was wrong and that "it" whatever "it" was would manifest itself somehow, someway to him. He was right and it did but not until later. He and Howie took some time off and looked for a new venture, one with promise and one in which they could use their selling skills. Then one day Howie said I found it. He found selling "timeshares" to be just what they needed to make a fortune once again.

While Howie was concocting the ins and outs for them in this new venture, Alan started to dabble in drug use. Minor dabbling to be sure, but using drugs was in the offering and would eventually prove to be his undoing. Just not yet.

The guilt and shame of what happened to them was inescapable and no matter how much money they made, no amount of wealth could or would erase the problems caused by doing what they did, then getting arrested, created. Little did Alan know the cosmic consequences he created were coming ever so much faster and closer.

Fortune was once again on their side and the venture into selling timeshares proved to be incredibly successful. They made more in this venture legally than they did before illegally. Only the selling of time shares, while legal, was a boon doggle for the unsuspecting. Eventually as they made more money scamming the unsuspecting, Alan began to lose his mind, his heart and his soul.

Drug use, to dull the pain was not what the doctor ordered but what Alan thought he needed. The more drugs he took the more he needed. It was in fact the loss of his character, his soul and his honor that was doing him in but he just didn't know it consciously. He only knew it unconsciously and it took the form of pain and suffering which lead to the drug use.

Who accompanied Alan on this perilous journey? Fear--not a person. Fear became his constant companion. Fear is unseen, but highly toxic. Fear accompanied Alan wherever he went and was with him when he did all those things he should not have been doing. Alan tried to hide his fear or prevent it from showing up behind drug use but he couldn't. No one can. Worse, he didn't know why he was afraid or of what.

As his troubles grew so did his drug use. The unhappiness that his work provided, proved too great and even the money, while fantastic, proved insufficient to stem his downward path. So, Alan in the belief he needed a change of direction, left the timeshare business and Howie, in favor of being a night club owner and a boxing promoter. This sudden change of direction did nothing to slow the onslaught of what he created for himself. It did not take long before the drug use caught up with him and low and behold gave rise to **"the decision"**.

EVALUATING HOW AND WHY TO MAKE THE RIGHT DECISION THEN MAKING IT

Getting arrested for using drugs was a minor charge, it was the charge of selling drugs that was the harsh one and carried the most time in jail, 15 years to life. Alan broke this harsh law. It took a while after getting arrested, for events to play out as they should. In this period of time, Alan had time to think.

First, he found a lawyer who specialized in criminal law and when asked by Alan what he should do, the lawyer looked at him in a pitying fashion and said," you have no chance of winning the case and

if you want to avoid jail you have to plead guilty".
Then tell them who your supplier is!

His wife said, "Alan my dear, sweet husband plead guilty and save all of us, we don't want to lose you". Even the Judge on the day of sentencing said to him, I am aware of the state's offer. If you accept, I will not put you in jail. But the condition for acceptance is you must turn in your supplier. If you don't plead guilty and turn in the supplier, I'll have no choice but to remand you to the custody of the sheriff who will transport you to Rikers Island, which at that time was maximum-security prison in upstate NY.

As it turned out Alan had 5 months to think about what decision he should make. He needed all 5. He could not have imagined so momentous a decision as this one. If he asked 1,000 people, all but one would have said turn on your supplier, 999 would have said take the deal and get away with it all. Going to jail is too dangerous, too risky and too frightening for you.

ALAN'S PROPHETIC SAYINGS

1. We create what happens to us. What happens to us is not random. Even if we don't know it, we are the cause and what happens is the effect;

2. Judgment creates separation. Judge another and see if an invisible wall is not erected between the two of you;

3. We are all one, there is no other;

4. Blame does not and cannot work as we are the cause of our own misfortunes;

THE DECISION AND ITS CONSEQUENCES

After considerable thought and introspection, Alan decided what decision he had to make and why. If I am to be honest with myself and accept responsibility for what I did I have no choice. He decided not to be a snitch, a rat and or a squealer. He chose instead to face the consequences of what he did. On the day set for trial he was asked by the Judge how do you plead? guilty or not guilty ? Not guilty would cause a trial to be held. The evidence of guilt as the detective said was overwhelming. It was and a jury found Alan guilty.

To this day, all Alan can remember is the Judge saying," you're sentenced to 15 years to life in prison, sheriff take him away." Off to jail he went, first to Rikers island where he spent a month getting beaten up regularly, and living in the worst conditions he could ever imagine. The food was awful, the inmates dangerous and violent to a one. Then as if to make matters worse, he was transferred to the Eastern Correctional Facility, a maximum-security prison.

Applying his sayings to his situation allows us to know why he made the decision he did. When he had to look at the cause of his predicament, he saw only himself. He was standing alone. The light of truth, justice and retribution was shining brightly but only on him. He made this fateful decision knowing full well what the consequences would be. With courage and confidence, he was doing the right thing for the right reason he accepted the consequences of his decision.

INNER PEACE
DESCENDS ON ALAN

After two years in a maximum-security prison where Alan barely survived without a major incident something totally unexpected but deserving happened. The first two years were not easy and there were several close calls but survive he did and then suddenly on a winters day while sitting in the prison yard with his back against a wall, he received "shakdipat" or as we say in English "inner peace".

Who among us does not want inner peace? Isn't this what we all strive to obtain? So was making **"the decision"** he made a blessing in disguise? Alan was in a maximum-security prison with the worst vile offenders the system has to offer, yet at the same time he was free from fear. Iron bars do not a prison make, or so the saying goes. Was the blessing he received unexpected or not anticipated by him making this decision? Yes! But the blessing was nevertheless bestowed on him and he deserved it.

If we were to have taken a survey 99% of those asked would have turned in the supplier and faced those consequences whatever they would have been. They had to have been different and perhaps could have been more severe but we just don't know.

What we do know is that Alan received the coveted blessing and got for his troubles what we all want and covet; freedom from fear. He has not had a day of fear since and as this article is written, Alan is a happy, healthy peaceful person who is not tormented by his past. He no longer needs drugs to ease the pain because the pain is gone.

SELF INFLICTED PUNISHMENT

In retrospect it's possible to opine that Alan inflicted the punishment he got on himself perhaps in the hope that by doing so he could atone for his sins. Well, we know he was punished but what we don't know is who was the actual punisher, why was he punished so harshly and whether the punishment fit the crime?

FORGIVENESS

Alan was forgiven by himself and then the governor of New York as he did receive executive clemency. He served 5 years only and now lives in Da Bronx, NY with a few friends and family at his side.

THE 3 "IN"'S WHICH CREATES THE SOLUTION

1. **_INQUIRY -_** What Alan did initially is to go within himself. The going within is called INQUIRY. This is not easy to do but when done fearlessly and fully it allows one to know where one erred, why and how. Knowing the where, why and how permits the second "in" to occur.

2. **_INSIGHT-_** Going within, penetrating the fog of denial and/or fear allows one to find the truth which when found is the key to insight. Once discovered, one can say "oh yes, now I recognize who I was when I did it, what I

did that was wrong, why I did those things; and all to show me the way home";

3. **_INTEGRITY-_** Once one and two are resolved, integrity is what is left. Integrity means I can be trusted to do the right thing for the right reason. I am a righteous person; I can be counted on

CONCLUSION:

Alan discovered that the happiness he sought for so long as well as the joy, contentment, and love of oneself can not ever be found outside of oneself. It is not in someone else or something else. If it were anyone of us could find it in sex, drugs, alcohol, money and someone else.

Alan took us to the answer. He went there fearless of the Archer Street thugs, and the consequences he brought on himself by making The Decision not to be a snitch of wrongful action. When he went within himself, he found as anyone of us can God, love and inner peace.

Written by Paul R Wiesenfeld

July 3, 2024

Copyright pending